To find an Ivory-Billed Woodpecker
...down Bayou de View

By Bobby Harrison

Illustrated by Joshua Caez

Dedicated to
my wife Norma Velazquez Harrison, my son Robert and
daughter Whitney with whom I've shared many nature adventures.

Text and Illustrations © 2005 by Bobby and Norma Harrison

All rights reserved. No part of this work may be reproduced or used in any form by any means – graphic, electronic, or mechanical, including photocopying, recording, taping, or any information storage and retrieval system–without written permission of the authors and publisher.

Designed by Bobby and Norma Harrison
Printed by College Press, Collegedale, TN
Printed in USA
First Printing

2 0 0 5 9 0 7 8 9 2
Library of Congress Control Number

ISBN 0-9771752-0-0

Published by Bobby and Norma Harrison
444 Shooting Star Trail, Suite T, Gurley, AL 35748
(256) 337-3368 • fax (256) 776-3734
e-mail: ivorybillwp@aol.com

Educators, fundraisers, gift buyers:
This book is available at special discounts when purchased in quantities.
For details, contact the authors.

Special Thanks

No book is produced or written by one individual. It is a collaborative effort among many people. Author Bobby Harrison and his wife Norma worked together to produce the story herein. Her insight and ideas were essential in the story line and production of this book.

Special appreciation is also extended to Barbara Curry who edited and re-edited this book numerous times. Also thanks to Joy Foster, Dr. Sandra Price, Dr. Dorothy Patterson, Barbara Embry, Tim Gallagher, Gloria Davis and Jeanette Kelso (my sister) for their editorial assistance and support.

Hey, kids!
Meet Bobby & Tim
  They will take you with them on a
              Nature Adventure . . .

Bobby

Tim

Dreams Really do Come True!
Bobby R. Hanson

                              . . . down Bayou de View

Once a year, Tim would travel all the way from New York to visit his cousin Bobby who lived in Arkansas. They both loved the outdoors and had great adventures together.

On one visit, their Uncle Scott took them to Gene's Barbeque for dinner. While they were there, they overheard some fishermen talking.

"Did you hear about that old kayaker who was in the bayou last week?" said one of the men. "He claims he saw a really big woodpecker that was much bigger than a pileated. He thought it might have been one of those ivory-billed woodpeckers, but he isn't sure."

A man with a long gray beard chuckled, "Ivory-bill! Those birds are supposed to be extinct."

Another fellow added, "I heard there was a woman from California at the White River refuge a few months back who said she'd seen one of those peckerwoods, also."

As the men talked, Bobby and Tim looked at each other. Their minds were busily at work. Then Bobby looked at Uncle Scott and said, "Uncle Scott, do you still have that old canoe you got from your neighbor, George?"

"Sure do, Bobby. What's on your mind?"

Tim jumped in and said, "We'd like to go look for that woodpecker."

"Woodpecker! What woodpecker?" Uncle Scott replied.

"The one those ole guys were talking about," Bobby said.

"Well," said Uncle Scott, "I don't see any harm in you boys getting out on the bayou and having a little fun, but don't get lost out there and be careful."

With excitement, Tim turned to Bobby and said, "We can get a compass from Uncle Fitz so we won't get lost and a pair of binoculars to look for the bird."

"Yeah," Bobby said, "and I bet our buddy Mr. Dan down at the pharmacy will put a first-aid kit together for us. Oh, I almost forgot the most important thing, FOOD! I'll fix lunch."

Tim burst into laughter and said, "You're always thinking about food, Bobby."

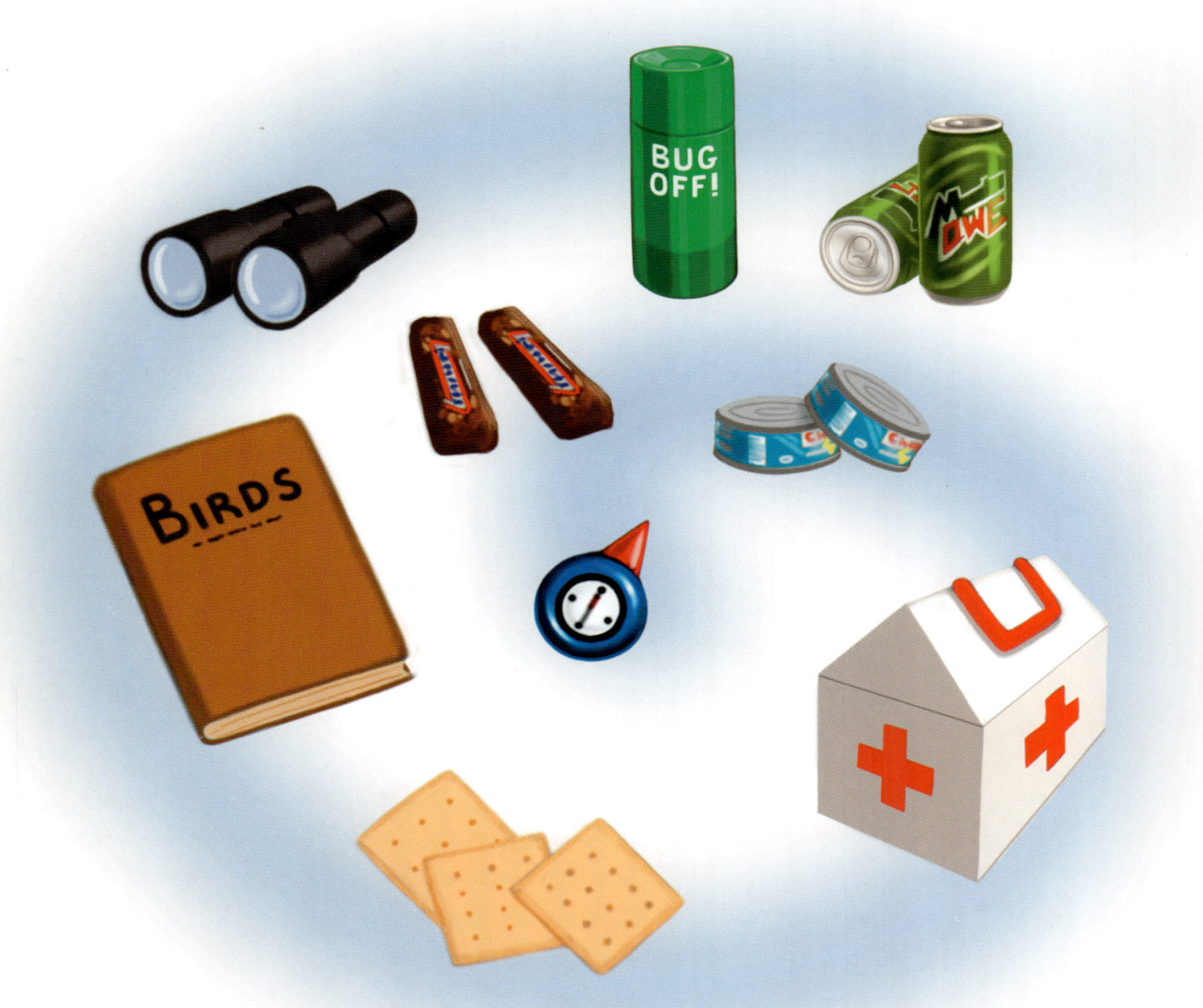

The next day, Bobby and Tim looked through their bird book. They wanted to see what the ivory-bill looked like.

Tim said, "Hey, this is it! The ivory-billed woodpecker, the one they think is extinct! It sure is a beautiful bird! It looks a lot like the pileated woodpecker, but it's bigger and it has a big white shield on its back when it clings to a tree."

"It looks like it has white suspenders going up its back and neck," Bobby giggled. "And look at that yellow eye."

Tim gasped, "What an awesome bird!"

Bobby asked, "Why didn't they believe that lady from California or that old kayaker?"

Tim replied, "Because no one else saw it at the same time, I guess. I wonder if there really are any ivory-bills out there."

"Oh, I don't know, but I would love to find out," sighed Bobby.

Early the next morning Uncle Scott dropped them off at Bayou de View with all their gear. The bayou was thick with huge trees, cypress knees, gnarled vines, mud, and lots of animals. This was just the kind of place that young boys love. Bobby and Tim loaded the canoe and headed into the swamp.

. . . and down the bayou they paddled.

Not far down the slough, Tim cried out, "Be careful, Bobby. LOOK OUT!"

They were heading toward a big pile of tree branches. Bobby jerked the canoe as he turned to look. In their excitement, they almost tipped over the canoe.

"WOW!" exclaimed Bobby. "That's one huge beaver lodge."

"More like a beaver mansion," said Tim. "Do you think it's dry inside?"

"It sure is, and it makes a really good hiding place. There are lots of beaver out here. Just look at all the trees they have chewed down. We'll need to explore that another time!" Bobby exclaimed. Suddenly, Bobby saw movement near the canoe.

"Did you see that? Was it a beaver?" Bobby said quietly.

"What? Where?" Tim replied.

They looked intently, trying to see what was darting just beneath the water around their canoe. Then, like a rocket, a furry animal sprang out of the water. It turned on its back and floated upside down right beside their canoe.

"It's an otter," laughed Tim.

"I wish we had a fish to give it," Bobby giggled, "but it'll find a fish before I ever could."

The otter followed them for quite a while. It swam around and sometimes swam under their canoe. This was the first time that either of them had seen an otter up close, and they were very excited.

As they drifted down the bayou, they kept a keen eye for anything that moved.

"Hey, there it is!" whispered Bobby.

"That's not it, silly! That's a pileated woodpecker. The back wing feathers are all black. An ivory-bill shows a lot of white feathers on its back."

Looking at the picture in the bird book again, Bobby agreed. "You're right, and I don't think it's quite big enough either."

As the pileated woodpecker hitched up the tree, Bobby and Tim paddled downstream and continued their quest to find the elusive ivory-billed woodpecker.

. . . and down the bayou they paddled.

Tree limbs stretched over the bayou, and logs lay tumbled all around. As Bobby and Tim kept a watchful eye, they saw something slither across one of the fallen logs.

"OOOh … look Tim!" Bobby stammered. "What kind of snake is that?"

"That's a banded water snake. Nothing to worry about. It only looks dangerous, but it's not poisonous," Tim replied.

"Yikes!" squealed Bobby, "But that one is! It's a cottonmouth!" He pointed to the hissing snake. It was curled around a branch with its white mouth agape.

"Let's get out of here!" urged Tim.

He didn't have to say it twice. They quickly paddled away and left the snakes behind.

"Look over there, Bobby. It's a raccoon."

"What in the world is it doing?" Bobby asked.

"It's washing its food. Looks like it's going to eat a crawdad for lunch. Did you pack that lunch like you said you would?" Tim inquired.

"Sure did, and I'm hungry. Let's stop and eat," Bobby said. They stopped paddling and scrambled onto the bank. Each got out a drink, some crackers, and a can of tuna. Of course, Bobby had brought his favorite candy bar and an extra one for Tim.

"That sure was good," Tim said.

"You bet," Bobby sighed as he patted his stomach. "I feel a lot better now."

"Well, don't you think we'd better get going? We have a lot of swamp to cover before we turn back," Tim said as they got back into their canoe.

Bobby answered wistfully, "I guess so. Maybe we'll still see an ivory-billed woodpecker."

"Look!" Bobby whispered. "There's a bobcat. Uncle Scott says there are plenty of them out here. He's probably looking for something to eat."

Teasing Bobby, Tim said, "I hope he's not thinking of eating us."

As they quietly giggled, the bobcat vanished behind the trees.

"I can't believe it. He's already gone," Bobby said with astonishment.

"He's a pretty sneaky creature. I can't see him anymore, even with my binoculars," Tim said as he held them tightly to his eyes.

Tim called quietly, "Look, Bobby, over there, at the deer! I hope that bobcat is far away by now."

"Me too," said Bobby. "They're so graceful and beautiful. I wouldn't want anything to happen to them."

Tim whispered, "I think they see us."

The deer looked in their direction, then sauntered away into the bayou mist.

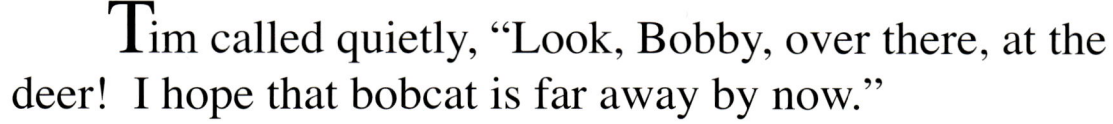

. . . and down the bayou they paddled.

It was now late in the day. Bobby and Tim had seen the bayou as few people do.

Then all of a sudden, Bobby saw a large black bird flying amidst the trees toward them. He pointed as he said, "Wow, look at that bird? It's huge! Is it another pileated woodpecker?"

Tim looked and said, "Yeah, probably another pileated."

Suddenly the bird tipped one wing down and the other wing up, turning on edge as it flew through the narrow spaces among the trees. Large white patches were visible on the back edge of both wings. With eyes wide in astonishment Tim shouted in excitement,

"NO WAY, LOOK AT ALL THAT WHITE!"

"IT'S AN IVORY-BILL!" The boys yelled at the same time.

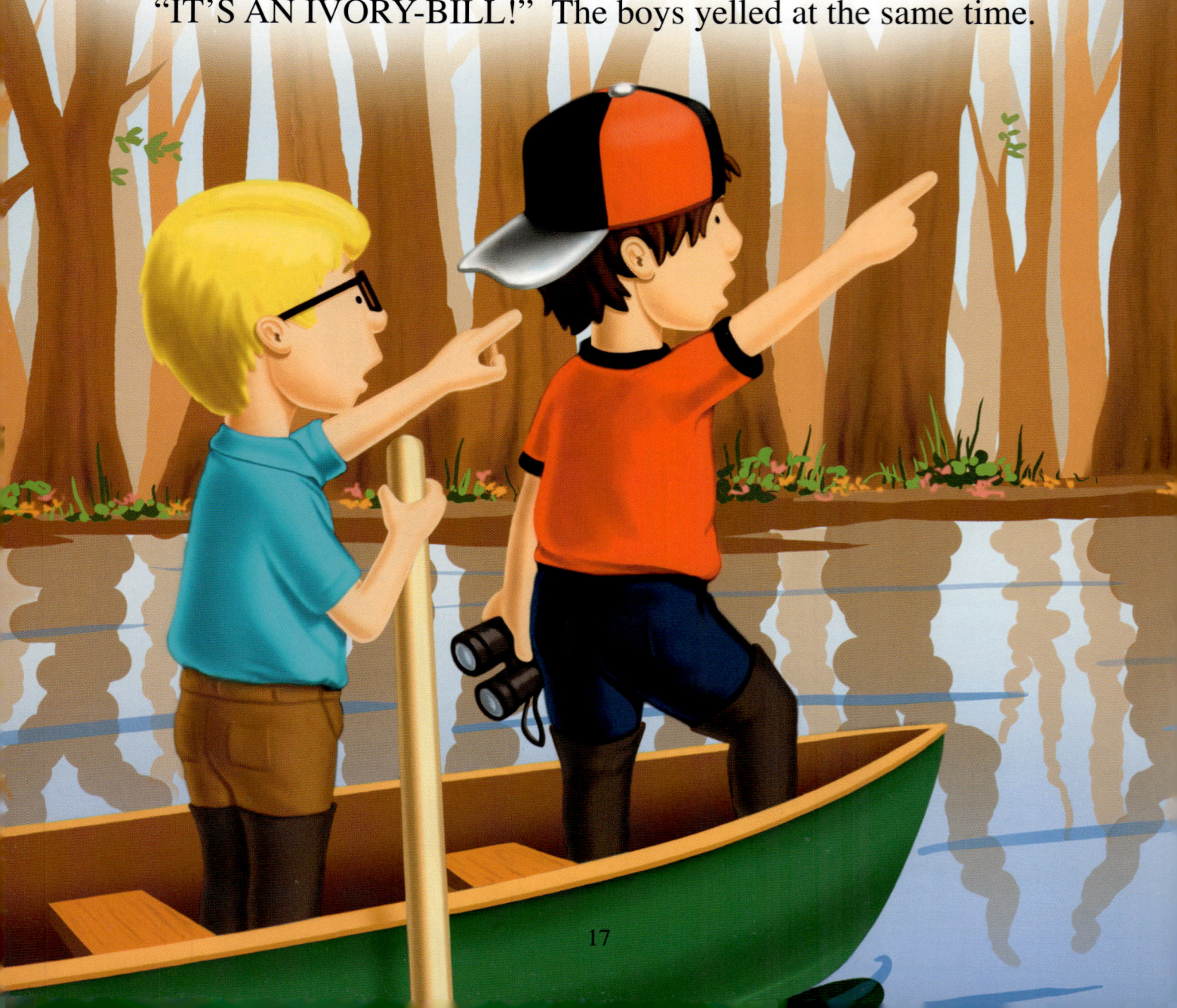

As the bird flew across the bayou in front of them, they had a perfect view. It flew fast and straight, and its massive white bill gleamed in the sunlight. Snow white feathers stretched along the back edge of it wings. It was the most spectacular bird they had ever seen. Almost as soon as they had seen the ivory-billed woodpecker, it disappeared into the swamp mist just like a ghost.

They could hardly believe their eyes. They sat in their canoe breathing heavily with hands shaking and hearts pounding. There really was an ivory-billed woodpecker in the swamp!

Their voices quivered with astonishment as they repeated, "I saw an ivory-bill! I saw an ivory-bill!"

Finally Tim asked, "Do you think Uncle Fitz and Uncle Scott will believe us?"

Hesitantly, Bobby answered as they turned their canoe to go back home, "I'm not sure. We're just kids, you know."

Bobby and Tim had seen the elusive ivory-bill, and they had seen it together.

Maybe they would tell their uncles, maybe not.

. . . then, back up the bayou they paddled.

At 1:15 pm, on February 27, 2004, after years of research and tracking down leads, Bobby Harrison (left) and Tim Gallagher became the first two qualified observers in sixty years to see an ivory-billed woodpecker at the same time.

Their discovery launched the largest, most intensive search ever undertaken for the ivory-billed woodpecker. The search was conducted by researchers from the Cornell University Lab of Ornithology, in Ithaca, New York; The Nature Conservancy; Oakwood College, in Huntsville, Alabama; the University of Arkansas Little Rock; and other organizations and agencies. The ensuing search resulted in eighteen sightings, two videos, and sound recordings that proved conclusively that the ivory-billed woodpecker still lives in the bottomland swamps of eastern Arkansas.

This iconic bird, a symbol of lost southern bayous and swamps, is now a symbol of hope for conservationists throughout the world. Efforts begun in the 1970s preserved vital habitat for the species, allowing it to survive. Major land acquisition and restoration efforts are currently underway to ensure the continued existence of this majestic species. Thanks to these efforts, the children of tomorrow may someday be able to experience the kind of southern swamp forest our earliest settlers enjoyed – swamps with massive, towering trees that harbor the magnificent ivory-billed woodpecker.